Your Name Will Be Israel

GENESIS
28-50

ALEX VARUGHESE

Copyright © 2021 by The Foundry Publishing®
The Foundry Publishing®
PO Box 419527
Kansas City, MO 64141
thefoundrypublishing.com

978-0-8341-4043-1

Printed in the
United States of America

Cover and Interior Design: J. R. Caines
Layout: Jeff Gifford

The internet addresses, email addresses, and phone numbers in this book are
accurate at the time of publication. They are provided as a resource. The Foundry
Publishing does not endorse them or vouch for their content or permanence.

10 9 8 7 6 5 4 3 2 1

Contents

THE *SHAPED BY SCRIPTURE* SERIES

The first step of an organized study of the Bible is the selection of a biblical book, which isn't always an easy task. Often people pick a book they are most familiar with, or books they think will be easy to understand, or books that, according to popular opinion, seem to have more relevance to Christians today than other books of the Bible. However, it is important to recognize the truth that God's Word is not limited to a few books. All the biblical books, both individually and collectively, communicate God's Word to us. As Paul affirms in 2 Timothy 3:16, "All Scripture is God-breathed and is useful for teaching, rebuking, correcting and training in righteousness." We interpret the term "God-breathed" to mean inspired by God. If Christians are going to take 2 Timothy 3:16 seriously, then we should all set the goal of encountering God's Word as communicated through all sixty-six books of the Bible. New Christians or those with little to no prior knowledge of the Bible might find it best to start with a New Testament book like 1 John, James, or the Gospel of John.

By picking up this volume, you have chosen to study the book of Genesis. You've made a good choice because this first book of the Bible lays a foundation for the rest of the story of God. Because the goal of this series is to illustrate an appropriate method of studying the Bible, instead of a comprehensive study of the entire book, our study will be limited to a few selected passages in Genesis.

In this volume, we will focus on seven stories from chapters 28–50. We have already taken up similar studies on stories from Genesis 1–11 and 12–27 in two previously published volumes in this series. We encourage you to gain a comprehensive understanding of Genesis by picking up these two volumes as well.

How This Study Works

This Bible study is intended for a period of seven weeks. We have chosen a specific passage for each week's study. This study can be done individually or with a small group.

For individual study, we recommend a five-day study each week, following the guidelines given below:

1	On the first day of the study, read the relevant passage several times until you become fully familiar with the verses, words, and phrases.
2	On the second day, we will review the setting and organization of the passage.
3	On the third day, we will observe some of the realities portrayed in the passage.
4	On the fourth day, we will investigate the relationship of the individual passage to the larger story of God in the Bible.
5	On the fifth day, we will reflect on the function of the story as we hear it today, the invitation it extends to us, and our response to God, who speaks through God's Word.

If this Bible study is done as a group activity, we recommend that members of the group meet together on the sixth day to share and discuss what they have learned from God's Word and how it has transformed their lives.

You may want to have a study Bible to give you additional insights as we work through the book of Genesis. Other helpful resources are *Discovering the Old Testament* and the two *New Beacon Bible Commentaries* on Genesis: Genesis 1–11 and Genesis 12–50, all available from the Foundry Publishing.

Literary Forms in the Bible

There are several literary forms represented throughout the Bible. The divinely inspired writers used various techniques to communicate God's Word to their ancient audiences. The major literary forms (also known as genres) of the Bible are:

- narratives

- laws

- history

- Wisdom literature (in the form of dialogues and proverbial statements)

- poetry (consisting of poems of praise, lament, trust in God, and more)

- prophecy

- discourses

- parables

- miracle stories

- letters (also known as epistles)

- exhortations

- apocalyptic writings

Within each of these forms, one may find subgenres. Each volume in the *Shaped by Scripture* series will briefly overview the genres found in the book of the Bible that is the subject of that study.

When biblical writers utilized a particular literary form, they intended for it to have a specific effect on their audience. This concept can be understood by examining genres that are familiar to us in our contemporary setting. For example, novels that are comedies inspire good and happy feelings in their readers; tragedies, on the other hand, are meant to induce sorrow. What is true of the intended effect of literary forms in contemporary literature is also true of literary forms found in the Bible.

THE BOOK OF GENESIS

Though it originates with God, the message of the biblical books comes to us through individuals whom God inspired to communicate his word to humanity. These individuals fulfilled their task by using their literary skill as speakers and writers of God's message. And they received the message in particular periods in the history of God's people—the Israelites in the Old Testament period, and the early Christian church in the first century BCE.

The books of the Bible clearly communicate truths about God, humanity, sin, judgment, salvation, human hope, and more. When we study a biblical book, we should do so with an awareness of its theological themes. So before we dive into Genesis, let's briefly summarize what we know about the book's authorship, literary forms, historical setting, broader context, literary structure, and major theological themes.

Who Wrote Genesis?

7

The book of Genesis belongs to a collection of five books that are known in the Jewish tradition as "the Torah" or "the Law." They are also called the Pentateuch (which means "five scrolls"). Besides Genesis, the Pentateuch includes Exodus, Leviticus, Numbers, and Deuteronomy. When it comes to authorship, some scholars hold to the traditional Jewish and Christian view that the Pentateuch is the work of Moses. Others, however, believe that the five books may have been composed by multiple authors.

Genesis is a collection of the Hebrews' oral traditions about creation and the beginning of human history. It also contains the stories of Abraham, Isaac, and Jacob—the three foremost ancestors of the people group that later came to be called Israel. The important thing is that while the authorship of Genesis (and many other biblical books) is frequently debated, we believe in the integrity of biblical books as we find them in the Bible today.

Literary Form

The book of Genesis is considered a narrative—that is, it is written mostly in prose and is made up of stories. Chapters 1–11 focus on creation and humanity as a whole; chapters 12–50 center on Abraham, Isaac, and Jacob. These stories deal with historical events from the family's history, interactions among the family members, and their interactions with outsiders. For this reason, most of the stories in chapters 12–50 belong to a subcategory of the narrative genre called *family stories*, in which one key individual plays a prominent role as the main character. In addition to family stories, Genesis contains genealogical lists of various people groups who lived in the ancient world (see chapters 5, 10, 25, 36, and 46).

Entering the Story

The stories in Genesis (and the rest of the Bible) are intended to draw readers in. Biblical narratives are never meant to remain ancient stories, and readers are never meant to be detached from them. Reading a Genesis story is like watching an exciting game in a stadium. Very rarely do we see people at sporting events sit still in their seats, unemotional and detached from the game. Most fans see themselves as part of the team—they cheer at every victory and yell at the players when they fail to execute the game plan. Likewise, the writers of Genesis invite us to enter into the story and become part of it. When we do, we soon discover that most of the narratives portray worlds that are much like our own. In the biblical characters, we see reflections of our own family quarrels and rivalries; our mistrust of God and others; as well as our doubt, pride, violence, deception, and hatred. Even the few individuals in Genesis who demonstrate integrity also have character flaws.

We may enter the story of Genesis and see ourselves and our own world through the lens of that story—but that does not mean that the story's purpose has been entirely accomplished. Most of the Genesis stories relate to some crisis. In Genesis, we often see God appearing in the midst of human crises and giving the characters guidance. When God's involvement is not explicitly mentioned in a particular story, we usually find it in preceding stories about the same character. Just like the people we know in our own lives, some of the characters in Genesis respond to God's voice and find resolution; others do not.

The stories in Genesis achieve their intended effect when readers respond to the invitation or challenge they encounter in each story. The characters we meet in Genesis and their interactions with a faithful God prompt us to imagine alternatives to our own crisis-ridden lives. How would a Genesis story change if the characters listened to God and took action to heal broken relationships and promote the well-being of others? How would our world look if we did the same?

The stories in Genesis invite us to embrace the life God intended for us when he spoke creation into being. We find the perfect model of such a life in Jesus. By following Jesus's example, and through our faith in him, we become God's new creation in the world. In doing so, we become who God originally created us to be. This is the intended effect of the stories in Genesis—personal transformation. As we read and study Genesis through this lens, we see the stories extend beyond their ancient context and become God's living Word to us today!

In this book, this is the approach we will take toward reading and studying Genesis. We admit that this method is somewhat different from that of many popular study materials, many of which seek to outline theological, moral, or ethical principles derived from biblical narratives and apply them to our own life circumstances today. Without denying the merit of such resources, we suggest that life *transformation*, rather than life application, should be the goal of our biblical studies.

Historical Context

In investigating the date and historical context of Genesis (or of any biblical book), we consider two separate but related issues. First, we examine the time and particular context (historical, political, cultural, social, and religious) in which the stories of Genesis took place. Second, we examine the date and the context in which the book was composed by its editors/compilers. Both of these factors are important for us to consider. The former helps us place specific narratives in specific settings, which is critical when it comes to comprehending the realities portrayed in the stories. The latter helps us understand how later generations would have heard and interpreted these stories.

Context of the Events in Genesis

Unfortunately, we cannot place the events in Genesis 1–11 in a specific historical period. This is because the events they describe occurred long before humans began documenting their history and civilization. We can only say that these stories come from the earliest period of human history and reflect the Israelites' beliefs about the origin of the world and humanity. These chapters also set the context for the stories of Abraham, Isaac, and Jacob in chapters 12–50.

We must also note that the stories in Genesis 1–11 are filled with gaps. Though the book flows seamlessly from one story to the next, we think the writers preserved only major incidents that changed the course of human history. For example, the writers cover the history of humans from creation to approximately 2000 BCE in only eleven chapters. However, it takes thirty-nine chapters (12–50) to tell the story of Abraham, Isaac, and Jacob—the three great ancestors of the people who would later become the Israelites. This disparity clearly suggests that the writers' primary goal was to tell their own story.

Most scholars agree that the stories in Genesis 12–50 come from the Amorite period in Mesopotamia, Syria, and Palestine (roughly 2000–1700 BCE). Scholars also believe that Abraham was part of a migratory movement of the Amorites from Mesopotamia into the Syria-Canaan region (see Genesis 11:27–32). Israel's ancestors lived as semi-nomadic people who pitched their tents in places where they found pasture for their flock. They were not part of an organized religious group—they worshipped God by setting up altars and offering sacrifices, and the head of the household performed the priestly tasks.

Though Abraham once participated in the Amorites' polytheistic religion, his encounter with the Lord led him to believe in the one true God, whom he called "Most High, Creator of heaven and earth" (Genesis 14:22). Scholars consider Abraham to be the founder of monotheism (the belief in one God). Abraham, his son Isaac, and his grandson Jacob worshipped God by setting up altars where God appeared to them during their travels.

Besides these fragmentary details, we do not know much about the setting of the stories in Genesis 12–50.

Context of the Writing of Genesis

Most scholars believe that the present form of Genesis was written in the sixth century BCE, when the Jewish people were living in exile in Babylon (after the Babylonians conquered Judah in 586 BCE and ended its political freedom). The exile threatened the future of the Jewish people and their identity as the covenant people of God in the world.

It is possible that the writer(s) of Genesis collected oral stories from the past and compiled them in written form with two goals in mind: (1) to provide the Jews in Babylon, as well as future generations, a foundational understanding of Israel's God as the creator and sustainer of the world; (2) to help the Jewish community understand their identity and mission in the world. We can summarize this mission and identity this way: though they are exiles living far away from the land God promised to their ancestors, they are still God's people. They belong to the family of Abraham, and they continue the mission God gave Abraham: to be an instrument of God's blessing to all peoples on earth.

As we hear God's Word today, it is important to investigate the context in which its books were written. While that context may be far different from our own, God's Word still speaks today, and we are able to experience Scripture in new, fresh ways. As we listen to the story of God in the Bible, we can experience God's Word as his "living Word" today.

Literary Structure

The fifty chapters in Genesis are organized into two major sections, comprised of chapters 1–11 and chapters 12–50, respectively.

First, chapters 1–11 contain several stories that deal with humanity as a whole. This section begins with two stories about God's creation of the world and humankind (chapters 1–2), followed by the story of humankind's first sin and its consequences (chapter 3). Chapter 4 shows us that violence has become a way of life for humanity. Chapter 5 is a genealogical list that traces the ancestry of Noah, who is the main character in the story of the flood, and who represents a new beginning for humanity in chapters 6–9. Chapter 10 is a genealogy of the descendants of Noah's three sons. Chapter 11 begins with another story of human rebellion and its consequences, and ends with another genealogy that traces the ancestral line from Noah (through his son Shem) down to Abraham (who is still known as Abram at this point).

Genesis 12–50 contain the stories of Abraham, Isaac, and Jacob. In 12:1–25:18, we find Abraham's stories. Though Isaac's family is introduced in 25:19–34, he is the protagonist in chapter 26 only. The rest of the stories in Genesis (chapters 27–50) largely center on Jacob, who becomes the father of the twelve tribes of Israel. Though Joseph's stories are prominent in chapters 37–50, Jacob remains in the background and plays a key role in the family's journey from Canaan to Egypt, where they settled after the deaths of Jacob and Joseph. Thus, the stories in chapters 37–50 serve to set the scene for the book of Exodus, which begins with the story of Israel's centuries-long enslavement in Egypt.

Major Theological Themes

Though it is mostly comprised of stories of families and individuals, Genesis also contains many significant theological themes. The fact that Genesis begins with the creation account suggests that the creation theme is central to the book. The following list describes other themes in Genesis and their connection to the creation theme:

Creation testifies to God's relational nature. Through his creation activities, God enters into a faithful relationship with the world (1:1–2:4).

God relates to his creation by blessing it. God's blessing is the source of creation's growth and well-being (1:22, 28; 2:3).

Humanity's mission is to be God's image in the world. We fulfill this mission through faithful relationship with God and the rest of creation (1:26–28).

Humans are the designated caretakers of creation. God gives humans the authority to serve as the shepherds of creation—not as despotic, exploitive, or destructive rulers (1:26–28).

God created Sabbath rest. By resting on the seventh day, God modeled a work-rest rhythm for creation (2:2–3).

To live in faithful relationship with God, we must live in obedience to him (2:15–17).

Human beings failed to be God's image in the world. This failure disrupted our relationship with God and with the rest of creation (3:1–24).

Disobedience and rebellion against God are a destructive, pervasive reality. God's judgment was the inevitable consequence of human sin (4:1–7:24).

In the midst of the judgment of the flood, God graciously created a new beginning for humanity through Noah and his family (6:9–9:17).

Noah's descendants resisted God's mandate to spread throughout the earth. As a result, God brought his judgment upon them (11:1–9; see also 1:28; 9:1).

God entered into a special covenant relationship with Abraham. God promised to bless Abraham with numerous descendants and to give those descendants a land of their own (12:1–3; 15:1–21; 17:1–27).

God's promise to bless Abraham's family (and all human families) is an extension of God's blessing on creation (see 1:22, 28).

God promised to bless "all peoples on earth" through Abraham (12:3). The covenant family's mission was to be an instrument of God's blessing to others.

Isaac and Jacob inherited God's covenant promises to Abraham (26:1–6; 28:10–22).

The future of Abraham and his family was shaped not only by God's promises, but also by the family's obedience to God. Several stories in Genesis 12–50 illustrate Abraham, Isaac, and Jacob's obedience to God's demands.

God remained faithful to Joseph, a member of the covenant family, and surrounded him during his difficult days in Egypt (39:1–23).

GENESIS 28:10-22

Genesis 12–50 preserves the stories of Abraham, Isaac, and Jacob—the three great ancestors of Israel. Jacob's story begins with the report of his birth (25:21–26). Though Jacob plays a key role in the stories of 25:27–34 and 27:1–28:9, 28:10–22 relates the story of his first solitary encounter with God.

This story is important for the Israelites for two reasons: (1) God spoke to Jacob and passed on the promises he had previously made to Jacob's grandfather Abraham (Genesis 12:1–3) and father Isaac (Genesis 26:3–4). Thus, Jacob became God's chosen heir to the covenant with Abraham. (2) The story establishes Bethel's historical significance as the site of God's first meeting with Jacob. This place later became the most important religious center in the northern kingdom of Israel.

According to Genesis 35:1–15, Jacob later revisited this site and set up an altar where he worshiped God with his whole family. Most of Jacob's stories in Genesis are encapsulated in these two encounters at Bethel (28:10–35:15).

WEEK 1, DAY 1

Listen to the story in Genesis 28:10–22 by reading it aloud several times until you become familiar with its verses, words, and phrases. Enjoy the experience of imagining the story in your mind, picturing each event as it unfolds.

The Setting

The stories of Genesis 12–26 provide the broader setting for Genesis 28:10–22. We learn from Genesis 12–26 that Jacob is a third-generation descendant of Abraham with whom God makes a covenant. God also promised to bless Abraham with numerous descendants, give them the land of Canaan, and bless all peoples on earth through them (12:1–3; 15:7–21; 17:1–22). Later, God passes the covenant promises he made to Abraham on to Abraham's son, Isaac (26:3–4).

The more immediate setting of this story is described in Genesis 27:1–28:9. Esau, Isaac's firstborn son, is the natural and legal heir to Isaac's deathbed blessing. However, Esau's brother Jacob steals the blessing in a scheme initiated by their mother, Rebekah. While Esau is hunting for wild game that he can cook for his father, Jacob disguises himself as his brother and receives the blessing intended for Esau. Isaac's blessing includes more than material prosperity; it also gives Jacob lordship over Esau. Most importantly, it includes the blessing God promised to Abraham (27:1–29). Once Isaac pronounces these words in God's name, they are irrevocable.

Once Esau discovers how Jacob took advantage of their father and deprived him of his blessing, he threatens to kill Jacob. Fearing Esau's reprisal, Rebekah persuades Isaac to send Jacob to Haran to stay with her brother. The event reported in 28:10–22 occurs when Jacob is traveling from his home in Beersheba to his uncle's home in Haran.

Keeping in mind the overview above, we will now dive into Genesis 28:10–22 — the story of God's encounter with Jacob.

The Plot

To discover the plot of Genesis 28:10–22, let's examine the passage by dividing it into six sections. **Below, summarize or paraphrase the general message or theme of each grouping of verses (following the pattern provided for 28:10–11, 12–13a, and 13b–15).**

1. Genesis 28:10–11

On the way to Haran from Beersheba, Jacob spends the night at a certain place.

2. Genesis 28:12–13a

Jacob has a dream while he is asleep.

3. Genesis 28:13b–15

God speaks to Jacob and makes several promises to him.

4. Genesis 28:16–17

5. Genesis 28:18–19

6. Genesis 28:20–22

What's Happening in the Story?

As we notice certain circumstances in the story, we will begin to see how they are similar to or different from the realities of our world. The story will become the lens through which we see the world in which we live today. In our study today, you may encounter words and/or phrases that are unfamiliar to you. Some of the particular words and translation choices for them have been explained in more detail in the **Word Study Notes**. If you are interested in even more help or detail, you can supplement this study with a Bible dictionary or other Bible study resources.

WORD STUDY NOTES #1

[1] The distance between Beersheba (in the southern part of Canaan) and Haran (in the southeastern part of modern Turkey) is approximately 600 miles.

[2] Verse 19 identifies the "certain place" as Luz, which Jacob then renames Bethel (meaning "house of God"). The distance from Beersheba to Bethel is about 60 miles; Jacob is thus only a few days away from home.

WORD STUDY NOTES #2

[1] According to some biblical narratives, dreams were one of the means by which God sometimes communicated with humans.

[2] Though some call this "Jacob's ladder," the Hebrew word translated "stairway" (which occurs only here in the Old Testament) most likely does not refer to a ladder.

1. Genesis 28:10–11

Jacob obeys his father's instructions (see 28:5) and sets out on a journey from his home in Beersheba to Haran.[1] At a certain place, Jacob stops to spend the night.[2] Instead of looking for lodging, Jacob decides to sleep along the roadside and use a stone to support his head.

2. Genesis 28:12–13a

While he is asleep, Jacob dreams[1] of a stairway[2] that connects earth with heaven and sees angels climbing up and down it. Jacob also hears God, who stands above the stairway (or "beside him"—see the NIV footnote), speak to him. Both the dream and God's voice confirm God's presence with Jacob in his journey.

_____

_____

_____

_____

_____

_____

3. Genesis 28:13b–15

God assures Jacob that he is the same God whom his grandfather Abraham and his father Isaac[1] worshiped and trusted. Thus, Jacob already has a relationship with this God through his ancestors. God also makes the following promises to Jacob:

1. God will give Jacob the land[2] Jacob leaves behind as he journeys to Haran (28:13). God's gift of this land to Jacob means that Jacob will eventually return home from Haran. God includes Jacob's descendants in the promise of the land. Though Jacob lives in fear of his brother's threat against him, this promise assures Jacob that he has a future (27:41).

2. Jacob's descendants will increase in population and become like the dust of the earth (28:14; see 13:16), spreading out in every direction.[3]

3. Jacob and his descendants will be instruments of God's blessing to all peoples on earth (28:14; see 12:3). This promise establishes the vocation of Jacob and his family: they are to mediate God's blessings to the world.

4. God will accompany Jacob in his journey (28:15). (See the promise, "I am with you," in Genesis 26:24; Exodus 3:12; Jeremiah 1:19; Isaiah 43:1–2; Matthew 28:20).

5. God will protect Jacob during his journey and return him safely to his homeland (God watching over Israel is a key theme in Psalm 121:1–8).

6. God will not leave Jacob until he fulfills the promises he made to him (28:15).

Practice the above pattern to summarize the world and reality that are portrayed in the following verses.

4. Genesis 28:16–17[1]

_____

_____

_____

_____

WORD STUDY NOTES #3

[1] God gives Jacob the same promises he made to Abraham and Isaac. These promises follow the same order in which they were given to Abraham in 12:1–3 (see also 13:15–17) and to Isaac in 26:3–4. Through these promises, God affirms his choice of Jacob as the heir to his covenant with Abraham. God's promises also confirm the blessings Isaac bestowed upon Jacob before Jacob left his home.

[2] That is, the land of Canaan.

[3] There is a close relationship between God's promise to Jacob concerning his descendants and God's blessing and mandate to all creation (see "be fruitful and increase in number; fill the earth" in Genesis 1:28).

19

WORD STUDY NOTES #4

[1] The Hebrew phrase translated "the house of God" is an expanded form of "Bethel"—the name Jacob gave to the place where God spoke to him in a dream (see 28:19). The phrase "the gate of heaven" means the pathway between heaven and earth. Both of these phrases convey humans' nearness and access to God.

WORD STUDY NOTES #5

[1] The Old Testament includes several reports of the setting up of a stone pillar (or pillars) as a memorial to covenant-making or an encounter with God (see Genesis 31:45, 35:14, 20; Exodus 24:4; Joshua 24:26–27). Old Testament law prohibited the use of such stones as an object of worship, which was a common practice among the Canaanite people (see Exodus 23:24; 34:13; Deuteronomy 7:5).

[2] In the Old Testament, pouring oil over someone symbolized the common being made sacred or consecrated for God's service.

WORD STUDY NOTES #6

[1] Since the law of tithing is not yet established, Jacob may be promising a one-time gift.

5. Genesis 28:18–19[1, 2]

_____

_____

_____

_____

_____

_____

_____

_____

_____

_____

6. Genesis 28:20–22[1]

_____

_____

_____

_____

_____

_____

_____

_____

_____

_____

_____

_____

_____

_____

Discoveries

Let's summarize our discoveries from Genesis 28:10–22.

1. Jacob, fearing his brother's anger and following his parents' instructions, left his home in Canaan and traveled alone to stay with his mother's brother in the distant land of Haran.

2. One night during his journey, God appeared to Jacob in a dream and assured him that he was the God of his ancestors.

3. God promised to give Jacob and his descendants the land of Canaan; to increase the number of his descendants; to spread them throughout the land; and to bless all peoples on earth through them.

4. God promised to be with Jacob, to watch over him during his travels, and to bring him home safely.

5. Jacob called the place of his encounter with God Bethel, meaning "the house of God," and consecrated it.

6. Jacob trusted that God would uphold his promise of presence and protection and provide for his basic needs during his travel.

7. Anticipating God's faithfulness, Jacob promised to have a personal relationship with God, to consecrate Bethel, and to give back to God a tenth of everything God would give him.

If you have a study
Bible, it may have
references in a
margin, a middle
column, or footnotes
that point to other
biblical texts. You
may find it helpful
in understanding
how the whole
story of God ties
together to look up
some of those other
scriptures from time
to time.

Jacob's Dream and the Story of God

Whenever we read a biblical text, it is important to ask how the text we are reading relates to the rest of the Bible. The theme of God's encounters with humans in critical times has an important place in the story of God. This theme is found in several places in the Bible in a variety of contexts; some of these include human disobedience, violence and oppression, hopelessness, and uncertainty. **In the space given below, write a short summary of how the theme of God's encounters with humans in critical times is utilized in each passage.**

1. Genesis 3:8–13

_____

_____

_____

_____

_____

_____

_____

_____

2. Exodus 3:1–10

_____

_____

_____

_____

_____

_____

_____

3. Joshua 1:1–6

_____

_____

_____

_____

_____

_____

_____

_____

_____

4. Isaiah 6:1–8

_____

_____

_____

_____

_____

_____

_____

5. Jeremiah 1:4–8

_____

_____

_____

_____

_____

_____

_____

_____

_____

6. Luke 1:26–38

7. Revelation 1:9–11

WEEK 1, DAY 5

Genesis and Our World Today

When we enter into the intriguing narrative of Genesis 28:10–22, the story becomes the lens through which we see ourselves, our world, and God's action in our world today.

1. In what ways does the story of Jacob fleeing from his home help us see our world today?

We live in a world where it is rare to seek forgiveness and reconciliation with those we have offended. We would rather distance ourselves from the brokenness we have caused than repair it by admitting our wrongdoing. For these reasons, Jacob's fear of his brother's retaliation, his guilt, and his loneliness are relatable to us today.

Following the above example, answer these questions about how we can understand ourselves, our world, and God's action in our world today.

2. What does Jacob's dream demonstrate to those who view God and heaven as distant realities that are far removed from our ordinary lives?

_____

_____

_____

_____

_____

3. Based on God's speech to Jacob, what was God's purpose in entering into our crisis-filled world?

_____

_____

_____

_____

_____

_____

_____

4. When God spoke to Jacob, he did not speak words of condemnation or judgment. What does this tell us about the way God relates to sinful humans?

_____

_____

_____

_____

_____

5. Based on Jacob's response to God, how should we respond to God's promise of his presence, protection, and faithfulness?

_____

_____

_____

_____

_____

Invitation and Response

God's Word always invites a response. Think about the way the theme of God's encounter with humans in critical times from Genesis 28:10–22 speaks to us today. What response does this scripture seek from us?

Jacob's story invites us to remember that our sinful and broken lives are not hidden from God.

The story also invites us to consider how to respond to the God who meets with us in the

midst of our brokenness with comfort and grace.

_____

_____

What is your evaluation of yourself based on any or all of the verses found in Genesis 28:10–22?

_____

_____

_____

_____

Dreams are one of the means by which God
sometimes communicates with humans.

GENESIS 32

In week one, we looked at the story of God's encounter with Jacob as he journeyed from his hometown, Beersheba, to Haran. Along the way, God made him the heir of his covenant promises to Abraham and Isaac. This week, we continue with Jacob's story.

After his first encounter with the Almighty (28:10–22), Jacob begins a relationship with God. From the stories in Genesis 29–31, we discover that Jacob continued to live in a world of deception for the next twenty years while he stayed with his uncle in Haran. Genesis 32:1–32 reports that on his way from Haran back to his home in Canaan, Jacob has another encounter with God. Jacob left Canaan fearing his brother's threats against his life. As Jacob returns home, he is certain he will have a life-threatening encounter with his brother Esau. During this critical journey, God meets Jacob and changes his identity by giving him a new name — Israel. After this life-changing encounter with God, Jacob is transformed into a person of humility who seeks to live in peace with others.

The reference to the appearance of angels (32:1) connects 32:1–32 to the story of Jacob's journey from Canaan to Haran (see 28:12). Genesis 32:24–29 describes a "man" wrestling with Jacob and Jacob's conversation with the man. However, Jacob calls the place of this encounter "Peniel," saying he "saw God face to face" (v 30). The presence of angels and of God himself show that God is keeping his promise to Jacob as he traveled to and from Haran (28:15; 31:3).

WEEK 2, DAY 1

Listen to the story in Genesis 32 by reading it aloud several times until you become familiar with its verses, words, and phrases. Enjoy the experience of imagining the story in your mind, picturing each event as it unfolds.

WEEK 2, DAY 2

GENESIS 32

The Setting

God's covenant promises to Abraham—to give him numerous descendants; to give him a land for those descendants; and to bless all peoples on earth through Abraham and his family—serve as the theological setting of the story of Genesis 32 (see Genesis 12:1–3; 15:7–21).

Isaac was born as the fulfillment of God's promise to give Abraham a son (17:9; 21:1). God passed his covenant promises on to Isaac (26:3–4), and then to Isaac's younger son, Jacob. God made the same promises to Jacob when, after deceiving his father and brother, Jacob journeyed from his home in Canaan. God also promised to be with Jacob, to protect and provide for his needs during his travels, and to bring him safely back to Canaan (28:10–22).

As God promised, Jacob arrived safely at his uncle Laban's house in Haran and began to work for him. After Jacob fell in love with Laban's younger daughter, Rachel, Laban promised that if Jacob worked for him for seven years, he would give Rachel to Jacob in marriage. However, Laban reneged on his agreement—when the seven years had passed, he instead gave Jacob his older daughter, Leah. Laban then told Jacob that he could have Rachel in exchange for another seven years of work (29:1–30).

Overall, Jacob served Laban for a total of twenty years (31:41). During this time, Leah bore six sons and a daughter, and Rachel bore one son. Additionally, Rachel's maidservant and Leah's maidservant each bore Jacob two sons (29:31–30:24).

After his twenty years in Haran, God commanded Jacob to return to Canaan. So one day when Laban was not home, Jacob left. When Laban learned of this, he pursued Jacob and caught up with him in the hill country of Gilead. After an angry exchange, Laban and Jacob made a covenant of peace and went their separate ways (31:1–55).

This is where we arrive at our story for this week. Genesis 32:1–32 describes Jacob's continued journey toward Canaan, where he anticipates a hostile encounter with his angry brother Esau, who had already threatened to kill him.

Keeping in mind the overview above, we will now dive into Genesis 32:1–32—the story of Jacob's life-changing encounter with God at the most critical time in his life.

The Plot

To discover the plot of Genesis 32, let's examine the passage by dividing it into seven sections. **Below, summarize or paraphrase the general message or theme of each grouping of verses (following the pattern provided for 32:1–2, 3–5, and 22–30).**

1. Genesis 32:1–2

God's angels meet Jacob on his way to Canaan.

2. Genesis 32:3–5

Jacob sends messengers to Esau seeking reconciliation.

3. Genesis 32:6–8

4. Genesis 32:9–12

5. Genesis 32:13–21

6. Genesis 32:22–32

Jacob wrestles a man and seeks a blessing from him. Afterward, Jacob receives both a blessing and a new name.

WEEK 2, DAY 3

What's Happening in the Story?

As we notice certain circumstances in the story, we will begin to see how they are similar to or different from the realities of our world. The story will become the lens through which we see the world in which we live today. In our study today, you may encounter words and/or phrases that are unfamiliar to you. Some of the particular words and translation choices for them have been explained in more detail in the **Word Study Notes**. If you are interested in even more help or detail, you can supplement this study with a Bible dictionary or other Bible study resources.

1. Genesis 32:1–2

After reconciling with Laban and continuing on his journey, Jacob seems to fear a hostile encounter with Esau. The fact that Jacob acknowledges the angels he meets as God's army[1] implies that he is aware of God's protection in his life. Jacob consecrates the site of this encounter by giving it the name Mahanaim.[2]

2. Genesis 32:3–5

Jacob sends messengers ahead of him to initiate reconciliation with Esau.[1] The message he sends to his angry brother demonstrates extreme deference—Jacob calls Esau his lord and refers to himself as Esau's servant. We do not know whether Jacob is using flattery or showing true humility here, but either way, he attempts to gain his brother's favor. Jacob also attempts to gain Esau's sympathy by referencing his years as a sojourner in Haran.[2] He mentions his wealth perhaps to assure Esau that he is not coming home to claim his inheritance. Jacob concludes the message with an appeal for Esau's favor.[3] It seems that the favor Jacob seeks from Esau is a reconciled relationship.

Practice the above pattern to summarize the world and reality that are portrayed in the following verses.

WORD STUDY NOTES #1

[1] The Hebrew word translated "camp" or "encampment" has military connotations.

[2] Mahanaim means "two camps," perhaps referring to God's camp and Jacob's camp. Mahanaim later became a Levitical city (Joshua 21:38) and a politically significant location in Israel's history (2 Samuel 2:8; 17:24, 27; 1 Kings 4:14).

WORD STUDY NOTES #2

[1] Esau had left Canaan and settled in Seir in the country of Edom, which is located southeast of Canaan (see 36:6–8 for the account of Esau's relocation to Seir).

[2] Jacob uses the Hebrew word for "sojourn" to describe his stay with Laban. In the Old Testament, a sojourner is a person without any legal rights.

[3] The Hebrew word translated "favor" also means "grace."

WORD STUDY NOTES #3

[1] A standard militia unit consisted of four hundred men (see 1 Samuel 22:2; 25:13).

3. Genesis 32:6-8[1]

_____

_____

_____

_____

_____

_____

_____

WORD STUDY NOTES #4

[1] Jacob's prayer follows a similar pattern to the lament psalms which appeal for God's help and deliverance from enemies (for example, see Psalm 31:15-16).

[2] The Hebrew word translated "kindness" also means "steadfast love," "covenant loyalty," "unfailing love," and "mercy."

4. Genesis 32:9-12[1,2]

_____

_____

_____

_____

_____

_____

WORD STUDY NOTES #5

[1] The Hebrew word translated "pacify" connotes the idea of making atonement.

5. Genesis 32:13-21[1]

_____

_____

_____

_____

_____

_____

_____

_____

_____

6. Genesis 32:22–30

Jacob sends his family and possessions across the Jabbok River[1] and stays behind, perhaps in an attempt to protect his family and possessions in case of a fight between him and Esau. That night, while Jacob is alone, a man wrestles[2] with him. Jacob may think his assailant is Esau—and so, even as the man dislocates Jacob's hip to force him to withdraw from the fight, Jacob wrestles with all his strength. As daybreak[3] approaches, the man urges Jacob to release him from his hold.

Realizing that his assailant is God himself, Jacob insists on a blessing as the condition of his surrender. Before he will bestow the blessing, God demands that Jacob reveal his identity.[4] God's demand is meant to force Jacob to admit the truth about himself—to acknowledge what others already know about him.

Jacob reveals his identity, thereby acknowledging that he is not a trustworthy person.[5] God quickly responds by giving Jacob a new name, and thus, a new identity—Israel.[6] God explains that Jacob's new name means that he persists in his struggles with humans and with God and succeeds. With this, Jacob will forever be known by the name Israel.

Though Jacob asks for God's name, God does not reveal his identity, but instead, blesses Jacob.

Jacob names this place Peniel[7] and acknowledges that though he encountered the Almighty face-to-face, God spared his life.

Practice the above pattern to summarize the world and reality that are portrayed in the following verses.

7. Genesis 32:31–32

_____

_____

_____

_____

_____

WORD STUDY NOTES #6

[1] The Jabbok River is located on the eastern side of Canaan (or the northern area of modern-day Jordan).

[2] The Hebrew word translated "wrestled" implies an intense struggle that leads to the participants getting dusty.

[3] Daybreak would mean that Jacob could see his assailant. The figure's urgent plea prompts Jacob to realize that his assailant is not a human being, but God—whom humans are not allowed to see (see Exodus 33:20).

[4] In the Israelite tradition, a person's name reveals a great deal about their character.

[5] The name Jacob means "he grasps the heel," which is language that connotes deception. The name could also mean "supplanter."

[6] The precise meaning of the name "Israel" is unknown. Some of the possible meanings include "God rules," "God strives," "God preserves," "one who strives with God," and "God protects."

[7] Peniel means "face of God."

Discoveries

Let's summarize our discoveries from Genesis 32.

1. God sent his army of angels to protect Jacob while he was on his way to Canaan.

2. Jacob sent his messengers to Esau, seeking a reconciled relationship with him.

3. Distressed by the approach of Esau and his four hundred men, Jacob devised a strategy to save at least half of his people and property.

4. In his desperate prayer for God's intervention, Jacob acknowledged God's blessings and faithfulness to him. Jacob also reminded God of his promise to prosper him and his descendants.

5. Jacob sent gifts to Esau in an attempt to pacify him and receive his favor.

6. While Jacob was alone at night, God entered into an intense struggle with him. Jacob persisted in the fight even after God dislocated his hip to force him to withdraw.

7. At the end of the struggle, Jacob admitted his true identity, and God gave him a new name, Israel.

8. After receiving God's blessing, Jacob named the place of his sacred encounter *Peniel*, meaning "the face of God."

9. In a physical representation of how God had weakened and humbled him in their struggle, Jacob continued his journey with a limp from his injured hip.

WEEK 2, DAY 4

Transformative Encounters and the Story of God

If you have a study Bible, it may have references in the margin, a middle column, or footnotes that point to other biblical texts. You may find it helpful in understanding how the whole story of God ties together to look up some of those other scriptures from time to time. Whenever we read a biblical text, it is important to ask how the text we are reading relates to the rest of the Bible.

This is not the only place in Scripture where we see God's personal impact on someone at a critical point in their journey. In the space given below, write a short summary of how the theme of God's encounter with humans to transform them is utilized in each passage.

1. 2 Samuel 11–12; Psalm 51

2. Mark 1:16–17

3. Acts 9:1–19

_____

_____

_____

_____

_____

_____

_____

4. Ephesians 4:17–24

_____

_____

_____

_____

_____

_____

5. 2 Corinthians 5:17–21

_____

_____

_____

_____

_____

_____

_____

_____

_____

_____

_____

WEEK 2, DAY 5

Genesis and Our World Today

When we enter into the intriguing narrative of Genesis 32, the story becomes the lens through which we see ourselves, our world, and God's action in our world today.

1. In what ways does the story of Jacob's return to his home help us see our world today?

For most of us, it is not easy to return to a place we have left due to relational conflict. Jacob's story encourages us to trust God's presence with us and take the necessary steps toward reconciliation, even in the midst of fear and apprehension about how we will be received by those we have offended.

Following the above example, answer these questions about how we can understand ourselves, our world, and God's action in our world today.

2. What do Jacob's efforts to appease Esau and his prayer for protection reveal about our human tendency to trust in our own resources even as we seek God's help?

3. What does God's struggle with Jacob tell us about the purpose of God's encounters with sinful humans today?

4. After his encounter with God, Jacob continued his journey as both a new person and a broken person. What does this tell us about the aftereffects of a life-changing encounter with God?

_____

_____

_____

_____

_____

Invitation and Response

God's Word always invites a response. Think about the way the theme of God's encounters with humans to transform them from Genesis 32 speaks to us today. What response does this scripture seek from us?

As Jacob was on his way to be reconciled with his brother Esau, God met him and transformed

him from being a deceiver to a person who prevailed in his struggle with God. Jacob's limp

was the visible mark of his life-transforming encounter with God.

_____

_____

_____

_____

_____

What is your evaluation of yourself based on any or all of the verses found in Genesis 32?

_____

_____

_____

_____

_____

_____

_____

_____

After his life-changing encounter
with God, Jacob is transformed
into a person of humility who seeks
to live in peace with others.

GENESIS 37

In this week's study, we continue with Jacob's story. In this chapter, the focus shifts to Jacob's twelve sons, and especially Jacob's eleventh son, Joseph.

Conspicuously missing from this chapter is any reference to God or God's covenant promise to Jacob's family. Instead, the story focuses on the deceptive, conflicted relationships of Jacob's sons—difficulties that mirror Jacob's own relationships before his life-changing encounter with God at Peniel.

At the center of the family's dissension are Joseph's dreams, which are the first of several dreams reported in Genesis 37–50. Genesis 37 marks the first dream report in the Bible which does not mention God appearing or speaking to the dreamer.

Ancient peoples thought that dreams gave mortals a glimpse into the divine realm and the gods' activities. People often sought the help of specialists to interpret what their dreams revealed about their future. In ancient pagan thought, the future revealed in one's dream was irreversible. The Israelites, however, believed that by having a relationship with God and appropriately responding to him, the future could be changed.

Joseph's dreams are fulfilled only later in the story (see 42:6; 50:18). The dreams introduced in our passage this week set the stage for the rest of Joseph's story.

WEEK 3, DAY 1

Listen to the story in Genesis 37 by reading it aloud several times until you become familiar with its verses, words, and phrases. Enjoy the experience of imagining the story in your mind, picturing each event as it unfolds.

The Setting

God's covenant promises to Abraham—to give him numerous descendants; to give him a land for those descendants; and to bless all peoples on earth through Abraham and his family—serve as the theological setting of the story of Genesis 32 (see Genesis 12:1–3; 15:7–21).

Isaac was born as the fulfillment of God's promise to give Abraham a son (17:9; 21:1). God passed his covenant promises on to Isaac (26:3–4), and then to Isaac's younger son, Jacob. Our study this week deals with Jacob's twelve sons, who would be the heirs to God's covenant promises and the mediators of God's blessing to all peoples on earth.

The geographical setting of this chapter is Canaan, the land God promised to give Abraham's descendants (though at the time of the events described in this chapter, that promise had not yet been fulfilled).

The more immediate setting of Genesis 37 is Jacob's family life in Canaan. Twenty years after deceiving his father and brother and fleeing from Canaan to Haran, Jacob returned home with his wives Leah and Rachel and their eleven sons. On the way, he had a life-changing encounter with God, followed by an emotional reunion with his brother Esau (Genesis 28–33).

Jacob later returned with his family to worship at Bethel, the place where God had met him on the way to Haran. From Bethel, Jacob and his family journeyed to the southern part of Canaan. On the way, at a place near Bethlehem, Rachel died while giving birth to Jacob's youngest son, Benjamin (35:1–20). After burying Rachel, Jacob continued his journey and arrived at his father Isaac's home in Mamre, near Hebron.

While Jacob and his family were living in Mamre, Isaac died, and Jacob and Esau buried their father in the family burial cave in the field of Machpelah (35:27–29; 49:29–32). Genesis 37 is set in the context of Jacob and his family's life in Mamre.

Keeping in mind the overview above, we will now dive into Genesis 37:1–36—the story of the conflict, hatred, violence, and deception in Jacob's family.

The Plot

To discover the plot of Genesis 37, let's examine the passage by dividing it into six sections. **Below, summarize or paraphrase the general message or theme of each grouping of verses (following the pattern provided for 37:29–36).**

1. Genesis 37:1–4

_____

_____

_____

_____

_____

_____

_____

2. Genesis 37:5–11

_____

_____

_____

_____

_____

_____

_____

3. Genesis 37:12–18

_____

_____

_____

_____

_____

_____

_____

_____

4. Genesis 37:19–24

_____

_____

_____

_____

_____

_____

_____

_____

_____

_____

5. Genesis 37:25–28

_____

_____

_____

_____

_____

_____

_____

_____

_____

_____

_____

6. Genesis 37:29–36

Jacob, believing that Joseph has been killed by a wild animal, is heartbroken. Meanwhile, the Midianites take Joseph to Egypt and sell him to Potiphar, one of Pharaoh's officials.

_____

_____

WEEK 3, DAY 3

What's Happening in the Story?

As we notice certain circumstances in the story, we will begin to see how they are similar to or different from the realities of our world. The story will become the lens through which we see the world in which we live today. In our study today, you may encounter words and/or phrases that are unfamiliar to you. Some of the particular words and translation choices for them have been explained in more detail in the **Word Study Notes**. If you are interested in even more help or detail, you can supplement this study with a Bible dictionary or other Bible study resources.

1. Genesis 37:1–4

Jacob and his family live in Canaan, where Jacob's sons tend the family's flocks. The seventeen-year-old Joseph becomes the object of his older brothers'[1] wrath when he gives their father a negative report about them (possibly pertaining to their misconduct while tending the flocks). Jacob seems to exacerbate the conflict between Joseph and his brothers when he displays preferential love for Joseph by giving him an ornate robe.[2] Thereafter, the older brothers' hatred prevents them from speaking peaceably[3] with Joseph. Thus, the opening verses of chapter 37 illustrate the fractured relationships within Jacob's family.

2. Genesis 37:5–11

As Joseph shares his dreams with his brothers, their hatred for him only intensifies. The brothers interpret Joseph's dream of their sheaves of grain bowing down to Joseph's sheaf as Joseph asserting superior status and authority over them. Though he might know that his brothers resent him, Jacob goes on to tell them and his father about a second dream, in which the sun, moon, and eleven stars bow down to him. Though Jacob rebukes Joseph for sharing his dream about the whole family paying homage to him, Jacob does not dismiss Joseph's dreams. As a recipient of divine dreams himself,[1] Jacob may believe that Joseph's dreams have some significance for the family's future.

WORD STUDY NOTES #1

[1] Dan and Naphtali are the sons of Rachel's servant Bilhah, and Gad and Asher are the sons of Leah's servant Zilpah.

[2] The Hebrew phrase translated "ornate robe" here refers to a dress coat with long sleeves. The familiar phrase "coat of many colors" is a translation based on the Greek and Latin Bibles.

[3] The Hebrew phrase translated here as "speak peaceably" can also be translated "speak a kind word."

WORD STUDY NOTES #2

[1] See Jacob's dreams in Genesis 28:10–22; 31:10–13.

Practice the previous pattern to summarize the world and reality that are portrayed in the following verses.

3. Genesis 37:12–18

_____
_____
_____
_____
_____
_____
_____
_____
_____
_____
_____

WORD STUDY NOTES #4

[1] The Hebrew term translated "dreamer" means "master of dreams."

4. Genesis 37:19–24[1]

_____
_____
_____
_____
_____
_____
_____
_____
_____
_____
_____
_____
_____

5. Genesis 37:25–28 [1,2,3]

_____

_____

_____

_____

_____

_____

_____

_____

_____

_____

_____

_____

WORD STUDY NOTES #5

[1] According to the Genesis genealogies, the Ishmaelites were the descendants of Ishmael, Abraham's son by Hagar (see Genesis 25:12–18).

[2] In verse 28, the terms "Ishmaelites" and "Midianites" are used interchangeably to refer to the same group.

[3] Later in Israel's history, selling a fellow Israelite as a slave would become a capital offense (Exodus 21:16; Deuteronomy 24:7).

6. Genesis 37:29–36

Reuben, who is unaware that the other brothers sold Joseph to the Midianite merchants, is grief-stricken when he does not find Joseph in the cistern. He is distraught about returning home without Joseph because, as the oldest son, he is legally responsible for the well-being of his younger brothers. The brothers successfully conceal their crime and, by showing Jacob Joseph's coat dipped in goat's blood, convince their father that Joseph has been devoured by a wild animal. The brothers' actions and attitude represent the breakdown of all family relationships.

Jacob goes into mourning[1] and remains utterly inconsolable. He is determined to spend the rest of his days in mourning until he joins his son in the grave.[2]

Meanwhile, the text reports that the Midianites sell Joseph to Potiphar, an Egyptian official. This suggests that Joseph's story will continue in Egypt, far away from his family in Canaan.

WORD STUDY NOTES #6

[1] Tearing one's clothes and putting on sackcloth were some of the ancient Israelites' mourning rituals.

[2] The Hebrew term translated "grave" is _Sheol_—the most common term in the Old Testament for the place of the dead. The Israelites thought of _Sheol_ as a place from which there was no return; a place of darkness; a place appointed for all the living (see Numbers 16:30; Job 10:22–23; 30:23).

Discoveries

Let's summarize our discoveries from Genesis 37.

1. The story of Genesis 37 portrays how the lack of peaceful relations within Jacob's family resulted in the older brothers' plot to harm Joseph.

2. Joseph contributed to the family's loss of peaceful relationships by provoking his brothers. First, Joseph gave his father a negative report about them; later, he told his brothers about his dreams, which led them to think that he was asserting lordship over them.

3. Jacob contributed to the family's loss of peaceful relationships by displaying preferential love for Joseph.

4. The older brothers contributed to the family's loss of peaceful relationships by harboring resentment, jealousy, and hatred toward Joseph.

5. The older brothers' plot to kill Joseph and their willingness to sell him to the Midianites indicate that they wanted to cut him off from the family.

6. The older brothers deceived Jacob into thinking that his beloved son Joseph had suffered a violent death.

7. Through their violence and deception, Jacob's older sons brought him inconsolable grief.

8. Though Genesis 37 does not describe God's words and actions in the midst of these events, God's covenant promises to Jacob (28:13–15) indicate that God was actively present with Jacob's family so that he might fulfill his plans and purposes for them.

WEEK 3, DAY 4

Harmful Plots and the Story of God

If you have a study Bible, it may have references in the margin, a middle column, or footnotes that point to other biblical texts. You may find it helpful in understanding how the whole story of God ties together to look up some of those other scriptures from time to time. Whenever we read a biblical text, it is important to ask how the text we are reading relates to the rest of the Bible.

Stories of destructive human plots are included in the Bible to show that our sinful world is the arena of God's redemptive work. **In the space given below, write a short summary of how the theme of humans plotting to harm other humans is utilized in each passage.**

1. Genesis 4:1–9

_____

_____

_____

_____

2. 1 Samuel 19:1–10

_____

_____

_____

_____

3. 2 Samuel 11:1–27

_____

_____

_____

_____

4. Jeremiah 11:18–23

_____

_____

_____

_____

_____

_____

_____

_____

5. Matthew 26:14–16

_____

_____

_____

_____

_____

_____

_____

_____

52

6. Acts 23:12–22

_____

_____

_____

_____

_____

_____

_____

_____

WEEK 3, DAY 5

Genesis and Our World Today

When we enter into the intriguing narrative of Genesis 37, the story becomes the lens through which we see ourselves, our world, and God's action in our world today.

1. What are some things in our world today that destroy peaceful relations between nations, ethnic groups, or family members?

International peace is destroyed by one nation's attempt to dominate another through military or economic strength. Tensions between ethnic groups stem from religious and cultural differences, and by claims that one group is superior to others. Family conflict often results from one family member speaking angrily or acting unkindly toward another.

Following the above example, answer these questions about how we can understand ourselves, our world, and God's action in our world today.

2. In what ways have we provoked strife in our relationships with people in our family, workplace, church, etc.?

3. In what ways do people plot to harm one another in our world today?

4. What are some things we can do to enjoy peaceful relationships with others (including those with whom we currently have strained relationships)?

_____

_____

_____

_____

Invitation and Response

God's Word always invites a response. Think about the way the theme of humans plotting to do harm to other humans from Genesis 37:1–36 speaks to us today. What response does this scripture seek from us?

God chose Jacob to be a mediator of his blessing to the world. However, because his older sons harbored resentment and hatred toward Joseph, Jacob's family did not live in peace. By removing their brother from their life, the older brothers destroyed the possibility of peaceful relationships and brought inconsolable grief to their father.

_____

_____

What is your evaluation of yourself based on any or all of the verses found in Genesis 37?

_____

_____

_____

_____

_____

_____

_____

_____

Though God seems absent in the midst of these events, God's covenant promises indicate that God is actively present.

GENESIS 39

Joseph's story in Genesis 37 ends with the tragic scene of Jacob's inconsolable sorrow at losing his beloved son Joseph. We then learn that the Midianites sold Joseph as a slave to Potiphar, an Egyptian official.

Genesis 39 picks up Joseph's story, which will progress through various scenes until the end of the book. The first major portion of Joseph's story in Egypt focuses on Joseph's successes, his troubles, and his eventual rise to prominence in Egypt. In this week's study, we will read of Joseph's initial successes and troubles in Egypt. Though God does not appear to Joseph or speak to him in these stories, God's presence with Joseph in both his triumphs and trials is a key theological emphasis of Genesis 39.

There are some parallels between Genesis 37 and 39. In both stories, Joseph is an innocent victim of powerful people (his brothers in chapter 37; Potiphar's wife in chapter 39). In chapter 37, Joseph's brothers throw him into a cistern because they hate him; in chapter 39, Potiphar imprisons Joseph because of his wife's false accusations. However, there is a significant difference between the two stories: while chapter 37 ends without hope for Joseph, chapter 39 ends on a positive note as it describes Joseph's success in prison due to God's presence with him.

Joseph's story in Genesis 39 has some slight parallels to an ancient Egyptian text, the Tale of Two Brothers. In this story, a woman attempts to seduce her husband's younger brother, and though he is guilty of no wrongdoing, she accuses the young man of improper behavior. Some scholars claim that Joseph's story is a later literary work based on the Egyptian tale, but there is no evidence for this. While the Egyptian story is from the twelfth century BCE, Joseph's story can be dated to the eighteenth century BCE.

The account of Joseph in chapter 37 is interrupted by the story of Judah and Tamar in chapter 38. Chapter 39 picks up by reiterating what we learned at the end chapter 37: the Midianites sold Joseph to Potiphar.

WEEK 4, DAY 1

Listen to the story in Genesis 39 by reading it aloud several times until you become familiar with its verses, words, and phrases. Enjoy the experience of imagining the story in your mind, picturing each event as it unfolds.

The Setting

God's covenant promises to Abraham—to give him numerous descendants; to give him a land for those descendants; and to bless all peoples on earth through Abraham and his family—serve as the theological setting of the story of Genesis 32 (see Genesis 12:1–3; 15:7–21).

Isaac was born as the fulfillment of God's promise to give Abraham a son (17:9; 21:1). God passed his covenant promises on to Isaac (26:3–4), and then to Isaac's younger son, Jacob. Thus, God made Jacob's family the heirs to his covenant promises.

The immediate setting of Genesis 39 is the story of Jacob's dysfunctional family in Genesis 37. With their words and actions, members of the family destroyed any hope of peaceful relationships. Joseph provoked his older brothers first by giving their father a negative report about them, and later, by describing his dreams to them—dreams that seemed to imply that the brothers would become subservient to him. Meanwhile, their father Jacob gave Joseph preferential treatment. These factors caused the older brothers to hate Jacob. Though his brothers initially plotted to kill Joseph, they ultimately sold him to Midianite merchants, who in turn took Joseph to Egypt and resold him to Potiphar, an Egyptian official.

Joseph's story in Genesis 39 is set in Egypt. Unbeknownst to Joseph, his arrival preceded a series of events that, in a later era, would end in Jacob/Israel's descendants also entering Egypt as slaves.

Joseph's arrival as a slave in Egypt took place sometime in mid-eighteenth century BCE. At that time, Egypt was controlled by a dynasty of Pharaohs known as the Hyksos—a foreign people who ruled Egypt for nearly two hundred years.

Keeping in mind the overview above, we will now dive into Genesis 39:1–23—the story of Joseph's early days in Egypt.

The Plot

To discover the plot of Genesis 39, let's examine the passage by dividing it into six sections. **Below, summarize or paraphrase the general message or theme of each verse or grouping of verses (following the pattern provided for 39:1, 2–6a, and 20b–23).**

1. Genesis 39:1

The Midianites/Ishmaelites took Joseph to Egypt and sold him to Potiphar, one of Pharaoh's officials.

2. Genesis 39:2–6a

Because of God's presence with him, Jacob was successful in everything he did and became Potiphar's most trusted servant.

3. Genesis 39:6b–10

4. Genesis 39:11–18

_____

_____

_____

_____

_____

_____

_____

_____

_____

_____

5. Genesis 39:19–20a

_____

_____

_____

_____

_____

_____

_____

_____

_____

_____

_____

_____

6. Genesis 39:20b–23

Because God was with him, Joseph was successful in everything he did while he was in prison.

_____

_____

WEEK 4, DAY 3

What's Happening in the Story?

As we notice certain circumstances in the story, we will begin to see how they are similar to or different from the realities of our world. The story will become the lens through which we see the world in which we live today. In our study today, you may encounter words and/or phrases that are unfamiliar to you. Some of the particular words and translation choices for them have been explained in more detail in the **Word Study Notes**. If you are interested in even more help or detail, you can supplement this study with a Bible dictionary or other Bible study resources.

1. Genesis 39:1

Joseph becomes a victim of human trafficking—his brothers sell him into slavery to the Midianites (also known as the Ishmaelites). The Midianites, in turn, transport Joseph from Canaan, his homeland, to Egypt, where they resell him to Potiphar, one of Pharaoh's officials.

2. Genesis 39:2–6a

God's[1] presence with Joseph enables him to prosper in Potiphar's house. Even Potiphar recognizes God's presence with Joseph and acknowledges God as the source of Joseph's success. Potiphar shows Joseph favor by appointing him as his personal attendant and trusted overseer of all his property. During the time of Joseph's service, God also blesses Potiphar's household and everything he owns. This prompts Potiphar to leave the household business he was normally concerned with in Joseph's capable hands.[2]

WORD STUDY NOTES #2

[1] We find the Old Testament's personal name for God—Yahweh, translated in English as "the LORD"—seven times in this story. Though Joseph himself does not mention God in these accounts, the writers present Joseph's story as a story of God.

[2] The phrase "except the food he ate" may mean that Potiphar is only concerned with what he eats, how it is prepared, who prepares it, and none of the other household matters. However, some scholars, citing an ancient rabbinic tradition, interpret this as a sexual innuendo in which the "food" is Potiphar's wife (see Joseph's words to Potiphar's wife in 39:8–9).

Practice the previous pattern to summarize the world and reality that are portrayed in the following verses.

3. Genesis 39:6b–10[1]

4. Genesis 39:11–18[1, 2, 3]

_____

_____

_____

_____

_____

_____

5. Genesis 39:19–20a[1]

_____

_____

_____

_____

_____

6. Genesis 39:20b–23[1]

Joseph experiences God's presence in the prison. Because of God's favor on Joseph, the warden appoints Joseph overseer of all of the inmates and activities in the prison. Joseph's God-given success also makes the warden confident that Joseph will faithfully perform the tasks assigned to him.

_____

_____

_____

_____

_____

Discoveries

Let's summarize our discoveries from Genesis 39.

1. Though Joseph was a victim of violence and human trafficking at the hands of his brothers and the Midianite merchants, God was with Joseph and gave him success in his Egyptian master's house.

2. Because he recognized that God was with Joseph and gave him success in everything he did, Potiphar appointed Joseph the overseer of his household.

3. Because of Joseph, God also blessed Potiphar's household and all his property. Potiphar then left everything in his household in Joseph's care.

4. Though Potiphar's wife commanded Joseph to have sex with her, he refused and instead stood firm in his commitment to his master and his conviction that adultery would violate God's standards.

5. Because he refused her forceful advances, Potiphar's wife fabricated a story about Joseph.

6. Potiphar imprisoned Joseph because of his wife's false accusations against the young man.

7. God was with Joseph in prison and showed him kindness. As a result, the prison warden appointed Joseph overseer of all the inmates and activities in the prison.

8. God gave Joseph success while he was in prison.

WEEK 4, DAY 4

Divine Presence in Human Troubles and the Story of God

If you have a study Bible, it may have references in the margin, a middle column, or footnotes that point to other biblical texts. You may find it helpful in understanding how the whole story of God ties together to look up some of those other scriptures from time to time. Whenever we read a biblical text, it is important to ask how the text we are reading relates to the rest of the Bible.

Joseph's story gives comfort and the assurance of God's presence to those who endure difficult days. **In the space given below, write a short summary of how the theme of God's presence in the midst of human troubles is utilized in each passage.**

1. Genesis 21:8–21

_____

_____

_____

_____

_____

_____

_____

_____

2. Exodus 3:7–12

_____

_____

_____

_____

_____

_____

_____

_____

3. Psalm 23:4

4. Psalm 46:1–11

5. Isaiah 43:1–2

6. Jeremiah 42:1–12

_____

_____

_____

_____

_____

_____

_____

_____

7. Matthew 28:16–20

_____

_____

_____

_____

_____

_____

_____

_____

8. Acts 18:9–11

_____

_____

_____

_____

_____

_____

_____

_____

WEEK 4, DAY 5

Genesis and Our World Today

When we enter into the intriguing narrative of Genesis 39, the story becomes the lens through which we see ourselves, our world, and God's action in our world today.

1. In what ways are conditions in our world similar to Joseph's experience as described in 39:1?

Our world is similar to Joseph's in that human trafficking and violence toward helpless young

people—particularly women and girls—is still an everyday occurrence. As ruthless and

oppressive forces treat them like commodities, victims of such heinous crimes are removed from

any support systems and suffer physical, emotional, and psychological trauma. These victims see

no hope for freedom or for a normal, peaceful life.

Following the above example, answer these questions about how we can understand ourselves, our world, and God's action in our world today.

2. Our trials may not be the same as Joseph's, but what troubles do we experience in our daily lives?

3. What are the consequences of choosing to live a life of integrity in our sinful world?

4. How can we know that God's presence is with us in the midst of our troubles?

_____

_____

_____

_____

_____

Invitation and Response

God's Word always invites a response. Think about the way the theme of God's presence in the midst of humans' troubles from Genesis 39:1–23 speaks to us today. What response does this scripture seek from us?

God was with Joseph in both his troubles and his successes. Though Joseph did not hear God's

voice, his triumphs in the midst of trials would have made him aware of God's presence

in his life. In the midst of his troubles, he remained loyal to both God and his earthly master.

_____

_____

_____

What is your evaluation of yourself based on any or all of the verses found in Genesis 39?

_____

_____

_____

_____

_____

_____

_____

_____

_____

_____

_____

Despite immense pressure, Joseph stood firm in his conviction that adultery would violate God's standards.

GENESIS 41:1-40

Joseph's story in Genesis 39 ends by noting God's presence with Joseph and Joseph's success while he was a prisoner in Egypt. Genesis 40 recounts Joseph's success as an interpreter of his fellow prisoners' dreams. Genesis 41 focuses on Joseph's interpretation of Pharaoh's dreams—a feat that moves Pharaoh to release Joseph from prison and appoint him an official in charge of the royal palace and the whole land of Egypt.

Though the stories of Genesis 40–41 do not explicitly mention God's presence with Joseph, they do refer to God and his work. Joseph confidently states to his fellow prisoners that the interpretation of dreams belongs to God (40:8). Joseph also mentions God several times in his speech to Pharaoh (41:16, 25, 28, 32). Pharaoh in turn recognizes Joseph as a person filled with the Spirit of God; Pharaoh also acknowledges God as the source of Joseph's interpretation (41:38–39). Thus, the stories of chapters 39, 40, and 41 are connected by the theme of God's hidden and mysterious activity in Joseph's life.

The story of Pharaoh's dream in Genesis 41 is similar to the story of Nebuchadnezzar's dreams in Daniel 2 and 4. In both cases, the ruler is troubled by his dreams (41:8; Daniel 2:3; 4:5). All the magicians and wise men (dream specialists) in Egypt cannot interpret Pharaoh's dream (41:8); likewise, all the dream specialists in Babylon cannot interpret Nebuchadnezzar's dreams (Daniel 2:1–13; 4:6–7). Both of these great and powerful rulers receive interpretations of their dreams from the most unlikely sources. In Pharaoh's case, the interpretation comes from Joseph, a young Hebrew man who had been sold into slavery by his brothers, and later imprisoned in Egypt because of false charges against him. In Nebuchadnezzar's case, the interpretation comes from Daniel, a young Hebrew man who is among the many Judean exiles in Babylon. Both Joseph and Daniel tell their rulers that God will reveal the meaning of their dreams (Genesis 41:16, 32; Daniel 2:28, 45). Both rulers acknowledge that the Spirit of God is at work in these young Hebrew men (Genesis 41:37–38; Daniel 2:47; 4:8). And in both cases, the Hebrew dream interpreters are elevated to high positions in the land where they live in exile.

WEEK 5, DAY 1

Listen to the story in Genesis 41:1–40 by reading it aloud several times until you become familiar with its verses, words, and phrases. Enjoy the experience of imagining the story in your mind, picturing each event as it unfolds.

WEEK 5, DAY 2

GENESIS 41:1-40

The Setting

God's covenant promises to Abraham—to give him numerous descendants; to give him a land for those descendants; and to bless all peoples on earth through Abraham and his family—serve as the theological setting of the story of Genesis 32 (see Genesis 12:1–3; 15:7–21).

Isaac was born as the fulfillment of God's promise to give Abraham a son (17:9; 21:1). God passed his covenant promises on to Isaac (26:3–4), and then to Isaac's younger son, Jacob. Thus, God made Jacob's family the heirs to his covenant promises.

The immediate setting of Genesis 41 is an Egyptian prison, where Joseph, Jacob's eleventh son, is being held. Joseph's older brothers hated him because of his dreams—dreams which seemed to imply that the brothers would become subservient to him—and because their father Jacob gave Joseph preferential treatment. Though the older brothers initially plotted to kill Joseph, they ultimately sold him to Midianite merchants, who in turn took Joseph to Egypt and resold him to Potiphar, an Egyptian official.

God was with Joseph in Egypt and gave him success in Potiphar's house—however, Joseph also encountered trouble there. Because Potiphar's wife falsely accused Joseph of sexual misconduct, Joseph was imprisoned. However, God was still with Joseph; the prison warden treated Joseph with favor and put him in charge of all the other prisoners and prison activities.

One of the gifts God gave Joseph was the ability to accurately interpret the dreams of two of his fellow prisoners—Pharaoh's chief cupbearer and chief baker. As Joseph predicted in his interpretation, Pharaoh restored the cupbearer to his former position and ordered the execution of the chief baker. Though Joseph implored the cupbearer to show him kindness and tell Pharaoh of his innocence, the cupbearer forgot Joseph as soon as he was reinstated. For two years, Joseph continued his life as a prisoner in Egypt.

Keeping in mind the overview above, we will now dive into Genesis 41:1–40—the story of Joseph's release from prison and his rise to a powerful position in Egypt.

The Plot

To discover the plot of Genesis 41:1–40, let's examine the passage by dividing it into seven sections. **Below, summarize or paraphrase the general message or theme of each grouping of verses (following the pattern provided for 41:1–8, 9–13, and 37–40).**

1. Genesis 41:1–8

Two years after Joseph successfully interprets the dreams of the chief cupbearer and the chief baker (two of his fellow prisoners), Pharaoh is troubled by two dreams. None of the dream specialists in Egypt can interpret them.

2. Genesis 41:9–13

Pharaoh's chief cupbearer suddenly remembers Joseph and tells Pharaoh of how he accurately interpreted dreams while they were in prison together.

3. Genesis 41:14–16

4. Genesis 41:17–24

5. Genesis 41:25–32

6. Genesis 41:33–36

7. Genesis 41:37–40

Pharaoh recognizes that God is the source of Joseph's discernment, and he acknowledges that Joseph is endowed with the Spirit of God. He then appoints Joseph his highest ranking official in Egypt.

WEEK 5, DAY 3

What's Happening in the Story?

As we notice certain circumstances in the story, we will begin to
see how they are similar to or different from the realities of our
world. The story will become the lens through which we see the
world in which we live today. In our study today, you may encounter words and/or phrases that are unfamiliar to you. Some of
the particular words and translation choices for them have been
explained in more detail in the **Word Study Notes**. If you are
interested in even more help or detail, you can supplement this
study with a Bible dictionary or other Bible study resources.

1. Genesis 41:1–8

Two years after Joseph successfully interprets the dreams
of the chief cupbearer and the chief baker (two of his fellow
prisoners), Pharaoh has two bizarre dreams.[1] In the first dream,
he sees seven healthy cows emerging from the Nile River,[2]
followed by seven scrawny cows. The scrawny cows then eat
the healthy ones. In his second dream, Pharaoh sees seven
dry heads of grain swallowing seven healthy heads. Pharaoh is
deeply troubled by the ominous nature of these dreams. The
fact that none of the dream specialists[3] in Egypt can interpret
them only intensifies his anxiety about what these visions
might mean.

2. Genesis 41:9–13

The chief cupbearer admits his shortcomings[1] to Pharaoh—
specifically, his failure to mention Joseph upon his reinstate-
ment to his position. The chief cupbearer may be afraid that
Pharaoh will be angry with him for withholding information
about Joseph's ability to interpret dreams. Though he does not
mention Joseph's unjust incarceration, the cupbearer reports
that he and the chief baker told Joseph their dreams, and that
Joseph's interpretation perfectly predicted the events that
followed.

75

WORD STUDY NOTES #1

[1] Especially because they center around the theme of the weak consuming the strong, Pharaoh understands that his bizarre dreams symbolize something ominous for Egypt's future.

[2] The Nile River was a symbol of Egypt's strength and wealth, and the Egyptians depended on it for their survival.

[3] "Magicians" and "wise men" were specialists who were trained in deciphering the meaning of dreams.

WORD STUDY NOTES #2

[1] The Hebrew word translated "shortcomings" means "sins."

WORD STUDY NOTES #3

[1] The literal translation of the Hebrew phrase rendered here as "God will give Pharaoh the answer he desires" is "God will answer Pharaoh's peace." Thus, Joseph tells the troubled Pharaoh that God will give him an interpretation that will bring him peace or wholeness (*shalom* in Hebrew).

Practice the previous pattern to summarize the world and reality that are portrayed in the following verses.

3. Genesis 41:14–16[1]

_____

_____

_____

_____

_____

_____

_____

4. Genesis 41:17–24

_____

_____

_____

_____

_____

_____

_____

_____

WORD STUDY NOTES #5

[1] The number seven, which occurs several times in Pharaoh's dreams and Joseph's interpretations, represented completeness or wholeness in the Old Testament.

[2] Jacob's declaration that "the matter has been firmly decided by God" conveys that the Egyptian gods are powerless to determine Egypt's future—that future is entirely under God's control.

5. Genesis 41:25–32[1,2]

_____

_____

_____

_____

_____

_____

_____

_____

6. Genesis 41:33–36

7. Genesis 41:37–40

Pharaoh approves of the famine management plan that Joseph proposes. He also admits that in all of Egypt, there is no one else like Joseph—a person in whom the Spirit of God is at work. Pharaoh also acknowledges that God is the source of Joseph's dream interpretation and his wise plan for the coming famine. For these reasons, Pharaoh puts Joseph in charge of his palace and officials—he declares that Joseph's power and authority in Egypt will be second only to his own.

Discoveries

Let's summarize our discoveries from Genesis 41:1–40.

1. Pharaoh was troubled by his bizarre dreams and by the fact that none of the dream specialists in Egypt could offer an interpretation.

2. Pharaoh's chief cupbearer told him that while he and the chief baker were in prison, Joseph interpreted their dreams, and his interpretations came true.

3. Pharaoh brought Joseph out of prison to interpret his dream. Joseph assured Pharaoh that God would give him an interpretation that would calm his troubled mind.

4. Joseph told Pharaoh that his dreams conveyed God's plans for Egypt's future, which included seven years of abundance followed by seven years of famine.

5. Joseph counseled Pharaoh to appoint a man with wisdom and discernment to oversee a crisis management plan. He proposed that during the years of abundance, officials should collect and store a portion of a harvest as a reserve for the years of famine.

6. Pharaoh recognized that Joseph was wise, discerning, and filled with God's Spirit. He then put Joseph in charge of his palace and officials, and gave Joseph a position second only to his own.

WEEK 5, DAY 4

Divine Foreknowledge and the Story of God

If you have a study Bible, it may have references in the margin, a middle column, or footnotes that point to other biblical texts. You may find it helpful in understanding how the whole story of God ties together to look up some of those other scriptures from time to time. Whenever we read a biblical text, it is important to ask how the text we are reading relates to the rest of the Bible.

The themes of God's knowledge of the future and the human response to God's revelation has an important place in the story of God. **In the space given below, write a short summary of how the theme of God's foreknowledge and our human response is utilized in each passage.**

1. Jeremiah 29:4–14

_____
_____
_____
_____
_____
_____
_____

2. Ephesians 1:7–10

_____
_____
_____
_____
_____
_____
_____

3. Ephesians 3:2–6

4. 1 Peter 1:3–16

5. Revelation 2:8–11

6. Revelation 21:1–5

WEEK 5, DAY 5

Genesis and Our World Today

When we enter into the intriguing narrative of Genesis 41:1–40, the story becomes the lens through which we see ourselves, our world, and God's action in our world today.

1. In what ways does our culture's perception of the future differ from Joseph's perception of the future?

Our secular world claims that humans control the future and can shape it with their plans and actions. The notion of God's involvement in humanity's future is alien to our world. Though we as Christians acknowledge that the future is in God's hands, in practice, we tend to follow the world's perspective. Joseph not only had faith in God's sovereignty over the future, but demonstrated that faith to Pharaoh by boldly asserting that the king's dreams revealed God's involvement in Egypt's future.

Following the above example, answer these questions about how we can understand ourselves, our world, and God's action in our world today.

2. Contemporary Christian orthodoxy does not consider dreams or dream interpretations to be a reliable way of discerning God's knowledge of the future—instead, the Bible is the record of God's self-revelation and plans for humanity. What are some of the plans for humanity that the Bible reveals (consider the scripture texts for Day 4)?

3. What response did God's revelation require from ancient audiences (consider the scripture texts for Day 4)?

Invitation and Response

God's Word always invites a response. Think about the way the theme of God's knowledge of the future and human response to God's revelation from Genesis 41:1–40 speaks to us today. What response does this scripture seek from us?

Joseph not only believed in God's knowledge of Egypt's future and his sovereignty over its affairs, but also advised Pharaoh to respond to God's revelation with bold action.

What is your evaluation of yourself based on any or all of the verses found in Genesis 41:1–40?

God never withdrew his presence
from Joseph's life.

GENESIS 45

Genesis 45 portrays the events that prompt Jacob to leave his home in Canaan and travel to Egypt to live near his beloved son Joseph. He makes this decision when his older sons, after going to Egypt to buy grain, return with the incredible news that Joseph is alive and has been made ruler of all of Egypt.

Jacob's decision to go to Egypt with his whole family is a significant event in the family's history. Jacob's sons and their decedents become residents of Egypt for the next 430 years—the last 30 of which are marked by slavery and hardship. Though a pharaoh in Joseph's time welcomes Jacob and his family to Egypt (45:16–20), a later pharaoh considers them a threat to national security—this later ruler suppresses the Hebrews' population growth and enslaves them (Exodus 1:8–14).

According to 46:3–4, God appears to Jacob, assures Jacob that he is with him, and promises to make him into a great nation in Egypt. God had already told Abraham that his descendants would be strangers and slaves in a foreign land—he had also promised Abraham that he would bring his people back to the land he had promised them (Genesis 15:13–14).

As we read the story of Jacob's decision to go to Egypt, we look back to God's speech to Abraham in Genesis 15 while also looking forward to God's redemption of the Israelites (as related in the early chapters of the book of Exodus).

WEEK 6, DAY 1

Listen to the story in Genesis 45 by reading it aloud several times until you become familiar with its verses, words, and phrases. Enjoy the experience of imagining the story in your mind, picturing each event as it unfolds.

The Setting

God's covenant promises to Abraham—to give him numerous descendants; to give him a land for those descendants; and to bless all peoples on earth through Abraham and his family—serve as the theological setting of the story of Genesis 32 (see Genesis 12:1–3; 15:7–21).

Isaac was born as the fulfillment of God's promise to give Abraham a son (17:9; 21:1). God passed his covenant promises on to Isaac (26:3–4), and then to Isaac's younger son, Jacob. Thus, God made Jacob's family the heirs to his covenant promises.

Joseph, Jacob's eleventh son, was sold into slavery by his brothers, who hated him and initially wanted to kill him (37:1–36). Joseph, who arrived in Egypt as a slave, spent his early years there in servitude, and later, after being accused of a crime he did not commit, was imprisoned (39:1–23). But because he was able to give an accurate interpretation of Pharaoh's bizarre dreams (which portended seven years of abundant harvest followed by seven years of famine [41:1–36]), Pharaoh elevated Joseph to be second in command over Egypt's affairs (41:37–57).

When the seven-year famine starts, Joseph's brothers travel from Canaan to Egypt to buy food. They do not recognize Joseph, who is in charge of Egypt's grain supply—however, Joseph recognizes them and accuses them of being spies (42:1–12). Joseph then devises a plan to force them to bring his younger brother to Egypt. After leaving Simeon in an Egyptian prison as collateral, the rest of the brothers return home. Jacob is reluctant to let Benjamin go to Egypt, but after much pleading and bargaining with their father, the older brothers take Benjamin with them to buy more grain (42:25–43:14).

Joseph is overwhelmed with emotion when he sees his younger brother Benjamin. He treats his brothers cordially and serves them a meal at his house (43:15–34). Joseph also devises a ruse to keep Benjamin in Egypt—he places his silver cup in Benjamin's grain sack. When the cup is discovered in Benjamin's sack, Joseph threatens to keep Benjamin as his slave in Egypt. This threat prompts Judah to plead with Joseph to have mercy on Benjamin—with deep emotion, he tells Joseph that their father may die of grief if Benjamin does not return home with them. Judah then offers himself as a slave in Benjamin's place.

Keeping in mind the overview, we will now dive into Genesis 45—the story of Joseph's emotional reunion with his brothers.

The Plot

To discover the plot of Genesis 45, let's examine the passage by dividing it into seven sections. **Below, summarize or paraphrase the general message or theme of each grouping of verses (following the pattern provided for 45:1–3, 4–7, and 25–28).**

1. Genesis 45:1–3

Joseph can no longer conceal his emotions—after sending his attendants away, he weeps aloud and reveals his true identity to his brothers.

2. Genesis 45:4–7

Joseph tries to comfort his brothers and reassure them that he will not retaliate against them. He tells them that God sent him to Egypt ahead of them so that he might save their lives during the seven years of famine.

3. Genesis 45:8–13

4. Genesis 45:14–15

5. Genesis 45:16–20

6. Genesis 45:21–24

7. Genesis 45:25–28

The news that Joseph is alive in Egypt renews Jacob's spirit, and he decides to go and see Joseph in Egypt.

What's Happening in the Story?

As we notice certain circumstances in the story, we will begin to see how they are similar to or different from the realities of our world. The story will become the lens through which we see the world in which we live today. In our study today, you may encounter words and/or phrases that are unfamiliar to you. Some of the particular words and translation choices for them have been explained in more detail in the **Word Study Notes**. If you are interested in even more help or detail, you can supplement this study with a Bible dictionary or other Bible study resources.

1. Genesis 45:1–3

Joseph, overwhelmed with emotion, orders his servants to leave him so that he can be alone with his brothers. (Perhaps he also does not want his servants to see him in such a vulnerable state.) Joseph then weeps aloud—not with sorrow, but with the joy that one might express when a missing family member—someone you've lost all hope of seeing again—suddenly returns. Joseph weeps so loudly that news of his cries reaches Pharaoh's palace.

Joseph's brothers are paralyzed with terror[1] when Joseph reveals himself to them. They struggle to answer Joseph's inquiry about their father—most likely because of their guilt and their fear of Joseph's retaliation.

2. Genesis 45:4–7

Joseph invites his brothers, who stand at a distance out of respect for his official position, to come near him. He again identifies himself as their brother Joseph. To confirm his identity, he reminds them of what they did to him twenty-two years earlier. However, Joseph is quick to comfort them and dispel their fears of his retaliation. He even declares that God used their betrayal to secure a future[1] for them and keep them alive[2] during the severe famine that will continue to ravage the land for another five years.

WORD STUDY NOTES #1

[1] The Hebrew term for "terrified" here conveys the panic and fear one might feel during enemy attack.

WORD STUDY NOTES #2

[1] The Hebrew term translated "remnant" here appears frequently in the prophetic books, where it refers to those who survive God's judgment, or those whom God keeps alive so that Israel might have a future.

[2] The Hebrew phrase translated "Save your lives by a great deliverance" here could also be translated "keep alive for you many survivors" (NRSV).

**Practice the previous pattern to summarize the world and
reality that are portrayed in the following verses.**

3. Genesis 45:8–13[1, 2]

WORD STUDY NOTES #3

[1] The meaning of the
title "father to Pharaoh"
is unknown—the phrase
does not appear in ancient
Egyptian sources. It may
refer to Joseph's role as
an advisor or counselor to
Pharaoh.

[2] We do not know the exact
location of Goshen, but it
was somewhere in the Nile
Delta.

_____

_____

_____

_____

_____

_____

_____

_____

4. Genesis 45:14–15

_____

_____

_____

_____

_____

_____

_____

5. Genesis 45:16–20

_____

_____

_____

_____

_____

_____

_____

WORD STUDY NOTES #6

[1] The Hebrew term translated "quarrel" here literally means "tremble" or "quake." Here, Joseph may be telling his brothers not to fear that he will change his mind or fear for their safety during their journey to Canaan and back. The NIV interprets this word as an admonition from Joseph to his brothers not to blame one another for what they did to him.

6. Genesis 45:21–24[1]

_____

_____

_____

_____

_____

_____

_____

_____

WORD STUDY NOTES #7

[1] The narrative uses the name Israel here in anticipation of Jacob and Joseph's reunion in Egypt. This reunion would pave the way for the family's new beginning in Egypt, where they would later be know as the Israelites (see Exodus 1:9).

7. Genesis 45:25–28

When they return to Canaan, the brothers do not rehearse the events that occurred in Egypt—they simply tell their father that Joseph is alive and is the ruler of all Egypt. Jacob is stunned at this incredible news, but remains skeptical. However, he becomes energized when he hears what Joseph told the brothers and sees the carts Joseph sent to transport him back to Egypt. Jacob/Israel[1] then not only believes the exciting news, but also proclaims his desire to reunite with Joseph in Egypt.

_____

_____

_____

_____

_____

_____

_____

_____

Discoveries

Let's summarize our discoveries from Genesis 45.

1. Joseph was overwhelmed with emotion when he revealed his identity to his brothers.

2. Joseph comforted his brothers, who feared he would retaliate against them for having sold him into slavery.

3. Joseph explained to his brothers that it was God, not they, who sent him to Egypt, and that God's plan was to give them a future by preserving their lives during the famine.

4. Joseph asked his brothers to tell their father about his high-ranking position in Egypt, and to convey his urgent request that Jacob bring his whole family and all his possessions to Egypt to live near Joseph.

5. In his message to his father, Joseph included a promise to provide for his entire family during the famine.

6. Joseph wept and kissed his brothers. The brothers who had once hated him and been unable to speak peaceably with him now engaged in conversation with their long-lost brother.

7. Through Joseph, Pharaoh told his brothers to bring their father and their families to Egypt, and he offered to give them the best land in the country.

8. As Pharaoh instructed, Joseph gave his brothers carts to bring his father and their families to Egypt. He also supplied provisions for their journey, including new clothing, and he treated Benjamin with special gifts.

9. Though Jacob was initially skeptical of the news about Joseph, he later became energized by the revelation and decided to go see Joseph in Egypt.

WEEK 6, DAY 4

Showing Grace to Enemies and the Story of God

If you have a study Bible, it may have references in the margin, a middle column, or footnotes that point to other biblical texts. You may find it helpful in understanding how the whole story of God ties together to look up some of those other scriptures from time to time. Whenever we read a biblical text, it is important to ask how the text we are reading relates to the rest of the Bible.

With stories like Joseph's, the Bible invites us to treat those who offend us not with retaliation or punishment, but with love, humility, compassion, and forgiveness—an act which is sure to result in reconciled relationships. **In the space given below, write a short summary of how the theme of showing grace to enemies is utilized in each passage.**

1. Genesis 27:41; 33:1–4

_____

_____

_____

_____

_____

_____

_____

2. 1 Samuel 24:1–22

_____

_____

_____

_____

_____

_____

_____

3. Matthew 5:43–48

_____

_____

_____

_____

_____

_____

4. Romans 12:14–21

_____

_____

_____

_____

_____

_____

5. Philippians 2:1–11

_____

_____

_____

_____

_____

_____

6. 1 Peter 3:8–12

_____

_____

_____

_____

WEEK 6, DAY 5

Genesis and Our World Today

When we enter into the intriguing narrative of Genesis 45, the story becomes the lens through which we see ourselves, our world, and God's action in our world today.

1. How does Joseph's treatment of his brothers (who severely mistreated him) compare with the way most people in our world (including Christians) treat those whom they consider to be their enemies?

We require those who mistreat us to apologize to us and admit their guilt; we demand justice.

Conversely, Joseph showed his brothers grace-he did not try to settle the score, demand

apologies, or seek admissions of guilt.

Following the above example, answer these questions about how we can understand ourselves, our world, and God's action in our world today.

2. In what ways do you think being vulnerable before others (as Joseph did) helps heal broken relationships?

3. Why is it important to view events in our lives through the lens of faith (as Joseph did), especially when we encounter those who have hurt us with their words and actions?

Invitation and Response

God's Word always invites a response. Think about the way the theme of treating enemies with love, humility, compassion, and forgiveness speaks to us today. What response does this scripture seek from us?

When Joseph encountered his brothers who had hated him, tried to kill him, and sold him into slavery,

he treated them with love, humility, compassion, and forgiveness. He did not demand that they

apologize or admit guilt. Because he viewed the events in his life through the lens of his faith

in God, he was able to be a grace-giver and reconciler rather than a vindictive brother.

What is your evaluation of yourself based on any or all of the verses found in Genesis 45?

We look back at
God's speech to
Abraham while also
looking forward to
God's redemption
of the Israelites.

GENESIS 50:15-26

The story of Israel (God's people in the Old Testament) began when God called Abraham and Abraham obediently responded by journeying to Canaan. After Abraham arrived in Canaan, God made a covenant with Abraham and promised to give the land to Abraham's descendants as their inheritance.

The book of Genesis ends with the fourth generation of Abraham's descendants — Jacob's sons and their families. As we read in chapter 45, Jacob's eleventh son, Joseph, was instrumental in bringing the family to Egypt. In chapter 50, we read of Joseph's death. Before he dies, Joseph makes his brothers promise to carry his bones with them when God leads them into the land he promised to their ancestors — Abraham, Isaac, and Jacob.

The last scene of the book of Genesis thus anticipates the stories that begin the book of Exodus: the stories of how the Egyptian enslave the Israelites; how God delivers his people from Egypt; and how God guides the Israelites through the wilderness toward the promised land. This Genesis scene also anticipates a happy ending to Joseph's story, in which he finally returns to his homeland (albeit in a casket), carried by the children of the brothers who sold him into slavery. Joshua 24:32 reports that the Israelites bury Joseph's bones at a place called Shechem in Canaan.

WEEK 7, DAY 1

Listen to the story in Genesis 50:15–26 by reading it aloud several times until you become familiar with its verses, words, and phrases. Enjoy the experience of imagining the story in your mind, picturing each event as it unfolds.

WEEK 7, DAY 2

GENESIS 50:15-26

The Setting

God's covenant promises to Abraham—to give him numerous descendants; to give him a land for those descendants; and to bless all peoples on earth through Abraham and his family—serve as the theological setting of the story of Genesis 32 (see Genesis 12:1–3; 15:7–21).

Isaac was born as the fulfillment of God's promise to give Abraham a son (17:9; 21:1). God passed his covenant promises on to Isaac (26:3–4), and then to Isaac's younger son, Jacob. Thus, God made Jacob's family the heirs to his covenant promises.

Joseph, Jacob's eleventh son, was sold into slavery by his brothers, who hated him and initially wanted to kill him (37:1–36). Joseph, who arrived in Egypt as a slave, spent his early years there in servitude, and later, after being accused of a crime he did not commit, was imprisoned (39:1–23). But because he was able to give an accurate interpretation of Pharaoh's bizarre dreams (which portended seven years of abundant harvest followed by seven years of famine [41:1–57]), Pharaoh elevated Joseph to be second in command over Egypt's affairs (41:1–57).

When the seven-year famine started, Joseph's brothers traveled from Canaan to Egypt to buy food. There, Joseph recognized them and accused them of being spies (42:1–12). Joseph then devised a ruse to force them to bring his younger brother to Egypt. After leaving Simeon in an Egyptian prison as collateral, the rest of the brothers returned home. Jacob was reluctant to let Benjamin go to Egypt, but after much pleading and bargaining with their father, the older brothers took Benjamin with them to buy more grain (42:25–43:14).

Joseph was overwhelmed with emotion when he saw his younger brother Benjamin and devised a ruse to keep him in Egypt. When Judah, with deep emotion, told Joseph that their father may die of grief if Benjamin did not return home with them, Joseph wept and finally revealed his identity to his brothers (43:15–45:7).

Joseph then sent his brothers back to Canaan with an urgent request that Jacob bring his whole family and all his possessions to Egypt. After an emotional reunion with Joseph, whom he had long thought dead, Jacob settled in Egypt with his family (45:8–47:12).

The immediate setting of Genesis 50:15–26 is Jacob's death in Egypt, his burial in the family burial cave in Canaan, and Joseph's return to Egypt with his brothers (50:1–14).

Keeping in mind the overview above, we will now dive into Genesis 50:15–26—the final interaction between Joseph and his brothers.

The Plot

To discover the plot of Genesis 50:15–26, let's examine the passage by dividing it into four sections. **Below, summarize or paraphrase the general message or theme of each grouping of verses (following the pattern provided for 50:15–18, and 19–21).**

1. Genesis 50:15–18

Joseph's brothers convey their father's deathbed request to Joseph: that he would forgive his brothers' sins.

2. Genesis 50:19–21

Joseph reassures his brothers by telling them that God took their plan to destroy him and used it to save many lives.

3. Genesis 50:22–23

4. Genesis 50:24-26

WEEK 7, DAY 3

What's Happening in the Story?

As we notice certain circumstances in the story, we will begin to see how they are similar to or different from the realities of our world. The story will become the lens through which we see the world in which we live today. In our study today, you may encounter words and/or phrases that are unfamiliar to you. Some of the particular words and translation choices for them have been explained in more detail in the **Word Study Notes**. If you are interested in even more help or detail, you can supplement this study with a Bible dictionary or other Bible study resources.

1. Genesis 50:15–18[1]

When Jacob dies, the older brothers begin to fear that Joseph might retaliate against them for all they did to him.[1] This may be why they deliver their father's deathbed request through a messenger—they were probably afraid to convey it to Joseph themselves. With his dying breath, Jacob asks Joseph to forgive his brothers for their sins and for the evil they did to him.[2] The brothers add to Jacob's request their own appeal for Joseph's forgiveness. They declare themselves servants of the God of Joseph's father, and thus, Joseph's spiritual brothers.

Joseph is moved to tears when he hears his father's final wish and his brothers' appeal for forgiveness. Once again, Joseph's brothers bow down before him, thus fulfilling the dreams that made Joseph the target of his brothers' hatred in the first place. In calling themselves Joseph's slaves, the brothers recognize Joseph's authority over them as well as their need for his forgiveness.

WORD STUDY NOTES #1

[1] In ancient Middle Eastern culture, siblings sometimes waited until their father's death to retaliate against each other (see Esau's words in Genesis 27:41).

[2] Jacob's request to Joseph includes words for "transgression," "sin," and "evil."

WORD STUDY NOTES #2

[1] The Hebrew phrase translated "you intended to harm me" here can also be translated "you intended evil against me."

2. Genesis 50:19–21[1]

Joseph attempts to comfort his brothers and dispel their fears. He reassures them that he would not dare to usurp God's authority as the sovereign judge of sinners. Joseph also makes it clear to his brothers that God used their attempts to destroy his life to instead preserve life—not only Joseph's life, but the lives of many others. Joseph promises to provide for his brothers and their children, thus reassuring and speaking kindly to those who once could not speak kindly to him (37:4).

Create your own brief summary or description of the reality portrayed in verses 22–23 and 24–26.

3. Genesis 50:22-23

_____

_____

_____

_____

_____

WORD STUDY NOTES #4

[1] The Hebrew word for "come" (in Joseph's declaration "God will surely come") literally means "visit." In some instances in the Old Testament, this verb is used to describe God visiting sinners to punish them; here, however, it connotes God visiting his people to save them.

4. Genesis 50:24-26[1]

_____

_____

_____

_____

_____

Discoveries

Let's summarize our discoveries from Genesis 50:15–26.

1. After Jacob's death, Joseph's brothers feared that Joseph would retaliate against them for the wrongs they committed against him.

2. Joseph's brothers delivered their father's deathbed request to Joseph: that he would forgive his brothers' sins and their evil treatment of him.

3. Joseph's brothers implored him for forgiveness of their sins as his spiritual brothers.

4. Joseph was moved to tears when he heard his father's deathbed wish and his brothers' appeal for his forgiveness.

5. Joseph's brothers bowed down before him and called themselves his slaves, thus recognizing his authority over them and their need for his forgiveness.

6. Joseph tried to dispel his brothers' fears by assuring them that he would not usurp God's authority as judge.

7. Joseph reassured his brothers that God worked through their evil actions to preserve the lives of many people. Joseph also promised to provide for his brothers and their children.

8. Before he died, Joseph anticipated that God would take the Israelites out of Egypt and lead them to the promised land.

9. Joseph died in Egypt at the age of 110. His body was embalmed and placed in a coffin for the Israelites to take with them to the promised land.

WEEK 7, DAY 4

God's Work in the Midst of Evil and the Story of God

If you have a study Bible, it may have references in the margin, a middle column, or footnotes that point to other biblical texts. You may find it helpful in understanding how the whole story of God ties together to look up some of those other scriptures from time to time. Whenever we read a biblical text, it is important to ask how the text we are reading relates to the rest of the Bible.

In the Bible, we see many instances in which God works through the evil in our world to enact his gracious plan for the good of all creation. **In the space given below, write a short summary of how the theme of God's mysterious work in the midst of evil is utilized in each passage.**

1. Psalm 27:1–5

_____

_____

_____

_____

_____

_____

_____

2. Isaiah 55:8–11

_____

_____

_____

_____

_____

_____

_____

_____

3. Jeremiah 29:1–14

4. Jeremiah 38:1–13

5. Daniel 6:1–23

6. Romans 8:28

WEEK 7, DAY 5

Genesis and Our World Today

When we enter into the intriguing narrative of Genesis 50:15–26, the story becomes the lens through which we see ourselves, our world, and God's action in our world today.

1. How do we tend to view the evil that mars our lives and our world today? How does this view compare to Joseph's perspective of the evils that affected his life?

We recognize the destructive power of evil and see its impact on our lives and our world—often, we feel helpless in the face of such forces. These feelings of helplessness can incline us toward resignation, hopelessness, and even the fatalistic perspective that evil is an inescapable reality. When evil occurs, we wonder where God is and what God is doing to stop it.

Joseph's perspective of evil was shaped by reflection on his past and present circumstances. When he considered his brothers' and their families' well-being and his own status in Egypt, he realized that God had unfolded his good and gracious plans for their family through his brothers' evil actions. When he reflected on the past, he recognized that God was with him in the midst of evil, including his slavery and imprisonment in Egypt.

Following the previous example, answer these questions about how we can understand ourselves, our world, and God's action in our world today.

2. Joseph's vision of reality was theologically informed by his faith in God's work in his life and the lives of those around him. Why is it important for us to have a theologically-informed perspective today?

_____

_____

_____

_____

_____

_____

_____

_____

_____

_____

_____

3. Why was Joseph confident that God would come and save the Israelites from Egypt?

_____

_____

_____

_____

_____

_____

_____

_____

_____

_____

_____

Invitation and Response

God's Word always invites a response. Think about the way the theme of God's hidden and mysterious work in the midst of evil in the world from Genesis 50:15–26 speaks to us today. What response does this scripture seek from us?

Joseph demonstrated his faith in God who works in and through the evil actions of humans to bring about his plans and purposes in the world. He saw the past, present, and future as the arena of God's good and gracious work for the well-being of all creation.

What is your evaluation of yourself based on any or all of the verses found in Genesis 50:15–26?

Joseph trusted God
to work through
humanity's evil actions
to bring about God's
covenant promises.

www.ingramcontent.com/pod-product-compliance
Lightning Source LLC
Chambersburg PA
CBHW081538040426
42447CB00014B/3413